FOREWORD

"When I first met Cornell Thomas it was through a mutual friend, we were featured guests on a radio program where I first heard the brilliance of Cornell's positive outlook on life and his genuine desire to help people through his first book "The Power of Positivity".

We immediately became friends and I've been able to not only mentor Cornell but also see him grow from an up and coming speaker to someone who now inspires thousand of people on a daily basis. In my 20+ years as a motivational speaker, author, and consultant myself I would have to honestly say that Cornell is a future world changer.

Cornell's positive mental attitude is all over his new book "The Power Of Me" - Army of One— fantastic stories, great success strategies, and practical positive thinking. If you grasp and act on the principles in this book, your life will continue to grow far beyond you could ever imagine. "Only those who risk going too far will ever know how far to go.

FOREWORD BY,

ROBERT E CRINER
SHARING A VISION SUCCESS NETWORK

Introduction

The most important person in your life is you. If your initial reaction to that sentence causes hesitation you're not alone. In fact, it took me about thirty years to understand this concept. Most of us are conditioned to take care of others before we take care of ourselves.

So when someone poses the question, "Who's the most important person in your life," we immediately start thinking about mom, dad, baby, and grandpa Joe. The problem with that mindset is without taking care of ourselves first we will never be able to help the ones we love.

Think about when you first get on an airplane. After the jostling around and trying to squeeze your carry on into a space the size of a Cheerio, the stewardess gives you the safety demonstration. I always used to think how crazy it was for me to put my oxygen mask on first before the old lady next to me.

Then I realized something. If I don't put my mask on first, I'd be a little too unconscious to help the sweet old lady that spent the flight telling me about her thirty cats. Make sense? I hope so, and if not, you came to the right place.

'The Power Of Me" isn't just a book. It's a guide to discover the inner strength we all possess. There are success stories, quotes, and - sorry to break it to you - homework. Think of it as practice before the big game of life, which we play every day.

I know you're good enough, and hopefully, after reading this book you'll know that you are, too.

Sincerely,
Cornell Thomas

Chapter 1

INTERESTED OR COMMITTED?

- **The perfect time is the moment you decide to take action.**
- **Don't be next, be *now!!***

I was at an author's convention recently where one of the speakers was John Assaraf. He was one of the contributors to the best-selling book, "The Secret" and is a successful entrepreneur with all sorts of billion-dollar business ideas.

While he was talking about his journey, he asked this question, "In terms of your book, business, or really most things that are deemed important in your life, are you interested or committed?"

That question immediately struck a chord with me because it's something I ask the players I coach on a daily basis. Are you willing to do whatever it takes to be the player you want to be? That question is usually answered with hesitation and sentence fillers like, "Um," and, "Uh."

With that pause, their answer is clear. There can be no hesitation when it comes to accomplishing your dreams. The famous proverb, "He who hesitates is lost," rings true in this situation. You might not lose everything, but you definitely won't win a grand prize, either. Fear, doubt, outside voices, lack of faith, and other crippling thoughts and habits hold us back from answering with a resounding YES! In listening and observing the journeys of many successful people, I have learned it's not the absence of fear that makes them successful; it's moving forward in spite of it.

Most of the time the person holding us back is the one we see when we look in the mirror. We refuse to commit because we put a cap on success.

From the moment we can comprehend, we're given mixed messages. We're told to dream big but be realistic. What?!? That's like telling someone to run fast but move slow. So we end up believing there's a ceiling to our success. That there's no possible way we could ever be a millionaire, play professional sports, or be an actor. The irony is that we watch people everyday doing just that. There are billionaires walking the same earth as you. We watch thousands of professional athletes on television. The Oscars take place every year. If they can do it, why not you? Are you interested in trying to be an actor or committed to being one?

If you're not committed to being great then you'll never be great. Even if you are committed, there's still no guarantee. So why take the leap? Why sacrifice partying with your friends, eating bad food every day, and God knows what else? You sacrifice because you're committed to accomplishing your dream; you're committed to making it happen. The sacrifice is when you take a day off. The sacrifice is when you take time away from your dream. It's not a sacrifice unless something you need is being taken away from you.

If I'm interested in a car, I might take it for a test drive, shake the dealer's hand, and then go home and look for another one. If I'm committed, I leave that lot in a new car. Don't leave your dreams on the lot.

Socrates

A young man asked Socrates the secret to success. Socrates told the young man to meet him near the river the next morning. At their meeting, Socrates asked the young man to walk with him toward the river. When the water was up to their necks, Socrates took the young man by surprise and ducked him into the water. The boy struggled but Socrates was strong and kept him there until the boy started turning blue.

When Socrates pulled his head out of the water, the first thing the young man did was gasp and take a deep breath of air.

Socrates asked, "What did you want most when you were there?"

The boy replied, "Air."

Socrates said, "That is the secret to success. When you want success as badly as you wanted the air, then you will get it. There is no other secret."

You need to figure out what it is you want and then ask yourself how bad you want it. It's not enough to just say it, you have to live it.

Chapter 2

ACTIVE DREAMING

- **The only dream too big is the one you don't believe in.**
- **Those afraid to soar will spend a lifetime watching others take flight.**

I'm wide-awake when I dream. It's not like I sleep with my eyes open or anything freaky like that, I just save my dreaming for when I'm awake.

When I sleep, my dreams are all over the place. I wake up trying to figure out why I was brushing my kindergarten teacher's teeth and why the heck we were in Paris. My dreams at night have no direction and no purpose.

Dreaming with your eyes open is what I call active dreaming. It's when you invest action into accomplishing your dreams. You can sleep all you want but it's not going to get you a job interview. Legwork is required to make dreams come true; they don't happen on their own.

Most dreams don't get accomplished because of the amount of work it takes to make them happen. So these dreams end up in a holding station where they eventually expire.

Can you imagine how many people take their dreams to the grave with them? One of those dreams could have changed the world. It could have been the cure for cancer or saved the environment. We'll never know until someone else steps up and dreams it for them.

I see it all the time; friends with brilliant ideas, and even better excuses why they can't pursue them. My work, my bills, my family…and the list go on. I could list a hundred reasons why writing a book when I did might not have been ideal, the biggest one being my first child.

What overrode the excuses was the reason I still wrote it. Writing a book was my dream. If it meant using the hours of 2am to 4am to write while the baby was asleep, I'd do it. The very first copy of my book hasn't been opened yet. It's for my son, Bryce, when he gets older. I'll tell him that in between his crying and exploding diapers, I had to sacrifice to get something done that I really wanted. I have the speech already memorized.

Your journey can't happen on the couch. It can't happen while you sleep the day away. Your dream happens when you start making it happen. It's the moment you realize that it's time to take action. It's when you watch your dream come true for someone else. You kick yourself wondering what if it was you. Why can't it be? Do you think there aren't other dreamers out there? You're reading one of their blogs right now. While you're waiting, someone else is working.

When you have a dream, go for it. Not after New Years but right now. Every journey starts with a single step. The kicker is we never know when we'll take our last one, so why not step toward something you love.

Active Dreaming Worksheet

Visualize something you want to accomplish within three different time frames. One you want to get done in the next couple of weeks, the next in three months, and the last in a year. This can be anything you want from joining a gym, to getting a new job. I want you to write out what these three goals are in the space provided below. Go ahead, I'll wait...

Goal 1 (14 Days)

Goal 2 (90 Days)

Goal 3 (365 Days)

Okay, now that we got that out of the way, you might be asking yourself how you are going to make this happen. We're going to do some brainstorming. For each goal, I want you to write a couple of things you need to start doing sooner rather than later to make them happen. Do not turn on the TV right now. Seriously, get this done.

Goal 1 (14 Days)

Goal 2 (90 Days)

Goal 3 (365 Days)

Okay, now what? GET TO WORK!! We're going to tackle the 14 day goal first. We're going to mono-task right now and only address the other two if something pops up in direct correlation to either one (and that might happen.) You have 14 days, so I have no clue why you're still reading this!!!

MAKE IT HAPPEN, CAPTAIN!!

Chapter 3

AS A MAN THINKETH

- **Convince the mind it's possible and it shall be just that.**
- **The master of his thoughts will be the master of his actions.**

One of my players told me to "You Tube" something the other day. Usually, when that happens it's basketball related, someone falling down a flight of stairs, or some other crazy scenario that would make the editors for "America's Funniest Home Videos" drool. So, imagine my surprise when I went to You Tube and entered the words "Earl Nightingale" and the title "As a man thinketh".

It was an hour long voice over (by Earl Nightingale) of the literary essay "As a man thinketh" by James Allen (circa 1902.) So, as I drove back and forth between gym, home, and all the other places I go during the day, I listened to it. The premise of the essay is what I talk about in almost every blog I write. A couple of my favorite quotes are:

"A man is literally what he thinks, his character being the complete sum of all his thoughts."

"Every action and feeling is preceded by a thought."

"Right thinking begins with the words we say to ourselves."

Sound familiar? Of course it does because every self-help

guru on the planet is saying the same thing today that James Allen was saying over a hundred years ago. So, if this was already known way before our time, why do so many people struggle with it? Why is there so much negativity in the world today? Is it really as easy as positive thinking? Is that all it takes?

Let me try to tackle some of these questions. People struggle with being positive the same way I used to struggle with Math. I would overanalyze every problem to the point that I couldn't see the answer right in front of me. I was looking for a complex solution that needed four different formulas - and in my case even a little magic - to work.

The other night I was talking to a good friend about this very thing. My friends always hit me with this excuse when it comes to being positive or a lifestyle change, "Easier said than done, Cornell." I don't buy that. I think it's a cop out. Why? Because it's being done every day, and if someone else can do it, why can't you?

Negativity often comes from frustration. The world is negative because, besides the obvious problems, there are a ton of frustrated people walking around; frustrated with their jobs, relationships, bodies, the neighbor's dog that barks at night, etc. You can only change your situation when you change your mindset. Now, I don't mean to imply that if you sit in your room thinking positive thoughts, money is going to fly into your apartment along with the beer you're too lazy to go downstairs and get from the fridge. The mind is the master of the body, not the other way around. Once your mind goes into action, your body will follow suit, and that's what a lot of us don't seem to comprehend.

If my mind was clear of all negative thought, I wouldn't be human. I would be a robot. The difference is how you handle those negative thoughts. I try to address them immediately:

- What's the problem?
- Is this really that serious?
- Is it life threatening?
- Is someone else going through something worse?
- Can I solve it?

By the time I get to the last question I'm already feeling better.

I love that James Allen says, "Right thinking begins with the words we say to ourselves."

What is your inner dialogue every day? I'm fat? I'm ugly? I'm not smart enough? I'm not good enough to play here?

How do you respond? Do you wake up and say, "I'm going to absolutely kill it today! Nothing is going to stop me from having a good day!" If we *are* what we think, why would we ever allow negative thoughts about ourselves?

Everything we do - even what we think is instinctive - involves thought. So make your thoughts positive, and your actions will be the same. This knowledge has been with us since way before 1902. Don't let another day pass without using it.

Chris Gardner

Chris Gardner struggled with homelessness while raising his son and working as a trainee stockbroker. He set up his brokerage firm, later selling it in a multi-million pound deal. He wrote an autobiography of his story, "The Pursuit of Happiness" (2006), which was made into a feature film describing his rags-to-riches story.

Chris Gardner's story is a perfect example of never quitting despite the odds that were stacked against him. If it weren't for his belief in himself, there would have been no story to tell. Passion fuels your pursuit of whatever you want out of life. Passion makes the impossible seem possible.

If you believe it, you will achieve it. Pursue what makes you happy and don't stop until you get it.

Chapter 4

YOGA

- **Your limits are whatever you make them**.
- **Bigger dreams take bigger actions.**

I was ten minutes into my first yoga class and I was sweating like I just played three games of basketball.

My whole body was shaking as I awkwardly tried to hold some animal-inspired position for what felt like an eternity.

Another issue was the 70 year old lady next to me who looked like she could fall asleep in this position. Not a bead of sweat trickled from her forehead.

Every person around me (mostly older women) had the same relaxed expression on their face. I couldn't believe they actually loved being tortured. At that moment my respect for yoga went through the roof.

I was just out of college and heard about some professional athletes doing yoga to help with their flexibility. I thought, "Hey, this shouldn't be that bad. I can almost touch my toes so I should be good." As bad off as I was physically, mentally I was even worse.

I didn't think my body could stretch as far as the teacher did, so I kind of compromised on each position. As soon as I felt a little discomfort, I stayed there. I didn't reach outside of my comfort zone; I lived in it.

My teacher, on the other hand, had different plans for me. She would suddenly appear at my side like Houdini and start making adjustments. I was too busy trying to figure out where she learned her ninja skills to notice her slowly pushing me past Comfort Point to the city of I'm-going-to-feel-that-in-the-morning.

With every class I attended my mind and body got stronger. The goals I started setting for myself in each position weren't comfortable, but they made me reach beyond what I thought was impossible.

Yesterday I listened to a passage from Les Brown about goals. He said, "Put something out there that makes you stretch." It struck me immediately because so often we're told to be realistic. In my mind, that is another way of saying, "Hey, you'll never accomplish this, so don't even try it."

Being realistic doesn't make you stretch. Being realistic doesn't push you. Being realistic sends you on the same path as billions of other people all over the world that are afraid to dream.

They're afraid to take the path less traveled, afraid to believe that anything's possible, afraid to look in the mirror and say, "I'm good enough," even when others are saying something different.

Don't take the bait. Don't go after the low hanging fruit. Stretch until you feel you can't go anymore, and then push yourself two inches farther than you thought you could.

The best dreams are still out there. Everyone has collectively decided to only go after what's at their eye level. The last time I checked, the stars were above us. Reach for them, even if it hurts.

Mono y Mono Worksheet:

I'm guilty of it, too., In fact, if there were such a thing as Multi-Taskers Anonymous, I would probably sign up right now; and I would probably do it while I was writing a practice plan, figuring out a blog, and feeding my son.

We live in a world where we want to do everything at once. Making more than one trip to the car to bring in the grocery bags is almost a sin (especially for us guys).

When your focus is on everything at once, it's hard to focus on anything. In this exercise we're going to pick 1 thing from our To Do list or one goal and knock it out of the park.

First things first; figure out what you're going to do. I want this to be like the picture of Drago on Rocky Balboa's bathroom mirror in "Rocky 4". If you haven't seen the movie, please make this your focus. Now, like we do almost everything, write it down.

Okay, now I want you to take a couple of minutes and brainstorm how we can get this done. Remember, no other goals matter right now. Ask yourself:

- Where do I start?
- What do I need to do right now?
- What's the time frame?
- Can it be done in that time frame?
- Am I capable of doing it? Which should be YES!

Alright! The goal is locked-in. Let's do this thing!!!!

Chapter 5

MAGIC PILL

- **Nothing handed to you will ever be as rewarding as what you've earned.**
- **The magic pill for success is realizing the magic is already inside of you.**

In households all over the world there are people on a quest for something that is not real. Late-night infomercials fuel the ignorance with testimonials from people that have somehow found the most sought-after thing since the fountain of youth. If curiosity is killing you right now (and you haven't read the title) it's called THE MAGIC PILL!

This magic pill is capable of everything. Do you want to lose weight without exercising? (DONE) Do you want to be a millionaire and never have to leave your house? (DONE) Do you want a personalized unicorn with your name bedazzled on its back? (DONE) For the record, the last one was completely fictional. I've never seen an infomercial for unicorns, but that's how ridiculous the idea of the magic pill is.

The legend of the magic pill continues to spread because, as the decades go by, more and more people feel entitled to success without actually working for it. I see this every day through basketball. I have seen players and their parents get upset with other kids for working harder than they do; like they are doing something wrong for wanting to get better. We live in a society of big dreams where people don't want to do the work to achieve them. This perpetuates the Magic Pill myth and allows it to continue growing.

I've been at games and have had parents, referees, and other players come up to me and ask how some of our players got to be so good? My answer has always been the same, "They work hard." You would think that those three words would satisfy their question, but they continue to ask more questions, like I'm leaving something out.

I actually want to start saying, *"Well, when they're twelve we put them in a laboratory where they're cut off from all human contact, and in that laboratory they can do nothing except play basketball or we won't feed them. Only the strongest ones survive."* I think if I said that they would probably accept my answer more easily.

I hate to be the spoiler for some of you reading this, but

THERE IS NO MAGIC PILL.

Success comes from a lot of things, but not one of those things is magic. I consider myself somewhat successful. I'm not a billion, million, or any other financial level that ends with aire, but I get to wake up and live basketball every day with people I care about. I don't sit in a cubicle all day. I don't have to put on a shirt and tie. I'm in basketball shorts and sneakers probably 350 out of 365 days a year, and the other 15 days I'm most likely in sweats.

If you have ever read my blogs, you know the struggle I had to endure through basketball, and life, to get to where I am right now. Countless hours of training myself and other people. Rejection after rejection, and some hard times off the court, as well. Bottom line is, it wasn't easy to get to this point.

I wouldn't trade any part of my upbringing, (outside of losing my father at an early age) if you paid me. It made me who I am. It made me appreciate the little things. It made me a problem-solver, not a problem-maker. I needed to go through the pain for this to happen. I can talk to kids about recovering from a major injury, about dealing with loss, being the worst player on a team, etc., because I've been there. I didn't need a magic pill to find success.

It saddens me that so many people are afraid to work for what they want. I watched about twenty minutes of the Olympic ceremony last night. Instead of focusing on the confusion that was taking place with one of the weirdest shows I've ever seen, I concentrated on the athletes.

The announcers would say, "This is her second Olympics," or some athletes were there even for their third. Twelve years of training just for the Olympics! No one just gave them a spot on the team, it had to be earned. The smiles on these athletes' faces before the biggest moment in some of their lives made perfect sense to me. It was their *journey* that made them appreciate the ceremony so much.

How could they not think about all of those grueling training sessions as they walked with their fellow countrymen and women holding their flags high?

The magic pill won't be found in some pharmacy. It will be accomplished through your hard work, determination, and effort to be successful, so stop looking for it.

J.K Rowling

J.K Rowling, the author of *Harry* Potter spoke to the graduating class of Harvard in June 2008. She didn't talk about success. She talked about failures. Her own, in particular. I absolutely love her quote.

"You might never fail on the scale I did," Rowling told that privileged audience. "But it is impossible to live without failing at something, unless you live so cautiously that you might as well not have lived at all—in which case, you fail by default."

She should know. The author didn't magically become richer than the Queen of England overnight. Penniless, recently divorced, and raising a child on her own, she wrote the first Harry Potter book on an old manual typewriter.

Twelve publishers rejected the manuscript! A year later she was given the green light by Barry Cunningham from Bloomsbury, who agreed to publish the book but insisted she get a day job because there was "no money in children's books. There is no magic pill.

J.K Rowling had to deal with rejection time and time again before she finally broke through. When we hear the word NO we automatically tell ourselves the fight is over. We've been conditioned since we were little that No is final. What we have to realize as dream chasers is not to take it personally. That No was meant to be. Remember everything happens for a reason, so move on and find that YES.

Chapter 6

STAIRWAY TO SUCCESS

- **There is no such thing as success without sacrifice.**
- **A path without obstacles is a path that leads nowhere.**

Every step toward greatness requires tremendous effort. When I think about people who are great in their respective fields I imagine them at stair one looking up at what seems to be an endless staircase. On their backs, they have a backpack full of weights that are meant to make the climb more difficult. In the beginning the bag is sometimes too heavy to bear. Some just walk back down the stairs and never try again. Others pause in their climb to take what they feel is a needed rest, and for whatever reason, fail to start climbing again. Then there are the great ones.

These are the ones that continue to climb the staircase even when they feel they can't take another step. They view every stair as one step closer to success. Instead of stressing about the number of stairs ahead of them, they take pride in knowing how many they have already climbed. When the backpack starts to weigh them down they take out all the things they don't need. They take out the fear, the insecurities, the what ifs, the critics, and after a while, all the weights are gone.

The great ones also realize one very important truth about the staircase, it never ends. To be truly great, they know that every stair is an opportunity to learn, and learning should only stop after you breathe your last breath. That continual search for knowledge and self-improvement separates them from all the others that have stopped climbing.

I have had the honor of meeting and learning from some truly great people in my lifetime. From world famous basketball coaches like Doc Rivers, and Mike Krzyzewski to sharing the mat and breaking bread with legendary fighter and UFC Hall of Famer, Renzo Gracie.

All of these great people have four major things in common. They have unbelievable drive, unbelievable passion, unbelievable humility and gratitude, and they are all lifelong learners. Not one of them believes they are a finished product, and that, my friends, is one of the biggest keys to being great.

On my staircase, I can't see the people in front of me or behind me. If I focus too hard in either direction I won't see the next step I have to take. I can't judge my climb by anyone else's because we're all different.

I don't just want to be a great coach; I want to be a great father, a great husband, a great mentor, a great humanitarian, a great sibling, a great friend, a great author, and the list keeps going. I don't want to be the next (insert name here) I want to be the first Cornell Thomas.

ROCKY WORKSHEET

Unless you've been living in a cave for the past thirty years, chances are you have either watched or heard of the "Rocky" movies starring Sylvester Stallone – there were SIX! Everyone loves an underdog story and Rocky Balboa was the epitome of a stereotypical underdog. He was an average fighter with above average heart and courage.

What made people fall in love with the character was that he overcame his own limitations against all odds. For me, it was no matter how hard Rocky got knocked down, he always got back up. It was almost as if he didn't know any other way.

Life is hard, ladies and gentleman. There will be days when you get hit with a haymaker. The question isn't _if_ you're going to get hit, it's what are you going to do when that hit comes?

What we cannot forget is that we've gotten ourselves up off the canvas before. Since before we can remember we've absorbed scrapes, bruises, and setbacks. When that punch comes, let your muscle memory do the work. Remember that you've been through it before and you can do it again.

Exercise:

1) Write down three times that you've hit the canvas hard and have gotten back up.

Now answer these two questions:

- Did you ever have any doubt you would recover?

- What did it take for you to get over it?

When that next punch comes, understand that you now have the blueprint. You can get up off the canvas because you've been there before!! Go get `em champ!

Chapter 7

IF

- **If you let your past define your present there is no future.**
- **The mind will provide the boundaries if you provide the excuses.**

If my father were still alive, there's a strong possibility that I would not have grown up without money. If I would have started playing basketball at an earlier age, who knows what kind of college I could have gone to right out of high school? If I would have never been injured, maybe I would just be finishing up my professional basketball career.

If I would have chosen a college that was closer to New Jersey, maybe my mom could have seen me graduate, and I would not have had to walk across the stage without my family in attendance. If I had started writing sooner, maybe I would already be releasing my second book. If, If, If.....

We live in a world of *if*. Millions of people use that one word as some type of bizarre time machine, only without the cool Delorean. One famous question you hear a lot is, "If you could go back and do it again, what would you do differently?"

If I could go back in time, I wouldn't. I believe in something called "the butterfly effect" which (without getting too intricate) simply states that if you change something small (like my basketball injury) it would have a ripple effect and change the course of something big (my life). In my case, that would be one hundred percent accurate.

Take away my injury and you take away thousands of people I never would have met. The basketball program I run for kids would not exist, and neither would all the great relationships I have made while coaching basketball. I honestly couldn't imagine my life without the people I know, care about and depend on now, so why would I want to go back? If you believe (like I do) that everything happens for a reason, you don't worry about if. You understand that there's a reason for everything that has occurred in your life, both good and bad. Both have shaped who you are right now.

Growing up without a lot of money has helped me appreciate the little things. I don't take things for granted because I never grew up with excess. My mom did her best to make the most of what we had and she did just that. I can talk to kids that don't have a lot because I've been there and did it without having to sell drugs or doing something illegal to make something of myself.

Why would I want to change that? Every day when I see kids that don't appreciate the iPhone, iPad, Xbox, or whatever else their parents bought them, I thank God for my upbringing. I tell our kids to thank their parents every day. Not just for material things but for the ride to practice, the roof over their heads, for running water, food, oh, and most importantly, for their lives.

When you focus on what could have been, you lose sight of what's still possible. In the movies, whenever a character wants to "go back" it's because nothing is working right in their lives. *If only I would have hit that home run in sixth grade my life would be completely different.* Really?! I hit a homerun in sixth grade and you know what changed? Nothing! I went home, did some chores and went to sleep. There was no parade and I didn't get the girl next door. (Luckily, because our neighbor was 50 with no kids.)

My quote yesterday was, "Sometimes you have to leave the past behind to stay present." Imagine how much you could get done today if you let go of yesterday? Don't worry about If, worry about right now.

Les Brown

Les Brown's life, itself, is a true testament to the power of positive thinking and the infinite human potential. Leslie C. Brown was born on February 17, 1945, on a floor in an abandoned building in Liberty City, a low-income section of Miami, Florida. He was adopted at six weeks of age by Mrs. Mamie Brown, a 38 year old single woman, cafeteria cook and domestic worker, who had very little education or financial means, but a very big heart. She had the desire to care for Les Brown and his twin brother, Wesley Brown. Les Brown calls himself "Mrs. Mamie Brown's Baby Boy" and claims, "All that I am and all that I ever hoped to be, I owe to my mother."

In the fifth grade, Les Brown was mistakenly declared "educably mentally retarded" and placed back in the fourth grade. He later failed the eighth grade due to inattention to school work, restless energy, and his teachers' failure to recognize his true potential. He was referred to as "D.T." for "Dumb Twin". The label and stigma held him back for years and severely damaged his self-esteem. Mamie Brown's belief in her son's ability to achieve whatever he set his mind to made a difference in his life.

"Her strength and character are my greatest inspiration, always have been and always will be."

Les Brown was determined and persistent in searching for ways to help his mother overcome poverty. His philosophy, "Do whatever it takes to achieve success," led him to become a distinguished authority on harnessing human potential and success. His passion to learn, combined with his hunger to realize greatness in himself and others, helped him to achieve greatness in spite of having no formal education or training beyond high school.

Other people will put a label on you but it's your fault if you start believing that label is who you are.

Chapter 8

I WILL

- **The only thing in your way is what you allow to stay there.**
- **See what you want to be and you'll be what you want to be.**

I will accomplish everything I set my mind and heart to. I will be great at what I do. I will believe in my abilities even when others don't. I will break the mold that so many willingly accept as their destiny. I will change the world. I will help others in need. I will work tirelessly to change millions of lives even if it's one at a time. I will.

Two of the most powerful words you can say to yourself. I will. The paragraph above is what I say to myself every day. If you notice it starts with me first and then branches out to everyone else. We tend to forget that the most important person in your life has to be you. If you're not taken care of mentally, physically, and spiritually, how could you ever help anyone else?

You have to believe what you dream, my friends. You have to break the sheep mindset that you're not good enough. That there's something wrong with believing you're great. Take all the numbers, equations, and any other statistical information the doubters throw at your dreams and toss them in the garbage. Numbers are just numbers, they can't measure a person's passion, heart, or determination.

When you say, "I will," you're saying that numbers don't matter. Imagine living your life by statistics. I can tell you right now if I did that, you wouldn't be reading this. I could have never played basketball, written a book, or aspired to motivate the masses on a daily basis. I'd sit home, too scared to leave the house because of some new report on how many people have passed away from bird droppings.

That's not living life. That's not believing you can do whatever you set your mind to. Fear has a funny way of disguising itself. Fear isn't just seeing a bear in the woods on your hike. Fear sometimes takes the form of the person you trust the most: yourself. When you look in the mirror, fear makes you turn away. Fear gives you excuses for every "I will" that you list, and then throws those things back at you to back up its' argument.

When I look in the mirror I only see myself. I don't see fear looking back at me because I'm no longer afraid. When I say positive affirmations, I mean them, and I don't give a damn who else is on board with me.

What do you say to yourself every day? Is it, "I will," or is it, " I won't," or, "I can't"? I'm telling you right now that you can. It's as easy as looking yourself in the eye and believing it.

I WILL WORKSHEET

Fear causes us to stop believing. Fear makes us question our greatness. Fear will make the possible seem impossible. One of the biggest problems with fear is it causes us to think negatively.

If you've been reading the previous pages in this book and not just looking at the cool pictures and quotes, by now you should know that *what we think, we attract*. When you allow fear to infiltrate your mind with negative thoughts, those usually end up being your results.

A big question that people ask me a lot is how do I keep negative thoughts from creeping inside my head when it comes to accomplishing my dreams? The answer isn't as complex as you might think. It just takes two simple words, "I Will."

Positive Affirmations will seem silly at first. The hardest thing to do sometimes is to be self-reflective; to look yourself in the eye and be 100% honest. So this is what we're going to do.

Step 1
- Find a mirror: any mirror will do, just make sure you can see your reflection. If you can't, you might be a vampire, and if that's the case you probably don't need my advice, or my blood for that matter.

Step 2

- Look yourself in the eye. Some of you will find this a little difficult to do. You might be a little insecure about your appearance, or yourself in general. Whatever you do, don't walk away from that mirror.

Step 3
- Think about something you want to accomplish. It could be something today, tomorrow, or weeks from now.

Step 4
- Look at yourself and say, "I Will…" Then finish that sentence with whatever you're thinking about in step 3. The last part of the sentence could be: get that job interview; be great today; write my book, etc. Anything you want to accomplish, say it right now.

Step 5
- Every day we're going to say this mantra. We're going to repeat it every day until we actually start believing it!

Chapter 9

PLAN B

- **A path without obstacles is a path that leads nowhere.**
- **The moment you think it's out of reach it will be.**

I don't have a plan B. I haven't had one in a very long time. Now that I'm thinking about it, I'd say my last Plan B was around my freshman year in college. From that point on, I wanted to be a professional basketball player and that was it.

In my mind, if I make a plan B, then I'm saying my original plan is not going to work. I'm admitting that I don't believe in my Plan A. Now mind you, I think a little bit differently than most people. I'm what you would call a grey thinker; I don't think in black and white. I used to daydream in almost every class I ever had. I dream big, and I cringe when I hear people say "be realistic." Those two words are Plan A killers worldwide.

What I used to hear a lot from friends and family was, "What if your plan A doesn't work? Then what do you do?" Before the smirk forms on their faces like they just beat me in a game of Connect 4, I simply say, "I don't *think* it will work, I *know* it will, and that's the difference between the way you think and the way I live. I live my life this way because I believe in the power of positive thought. I believe that what you think and feel is truly what you attract. I also believe in my work ethic. I believe in hard work. I believe that my plan A will work because I'm going to bust my butt to make it work."

If you put in the work, if your perspiration matches your aspiration, then why can't your plan A be the only plan you need? If you believe in who you are, and work at accomplishing your goals, there will be no ceiling to what you can accomplish. The problem is when you hear the negative voices (even your own) question your plan, the seed starts to get planted that maybe you should have a backup plan. Maybe passing the bar exam isn't "realistic." Guess what? Neither was breaking a 4 minute mile back in the day, but no one took into account that Sir Roger Bannister's plan was breaking that milestone (which he did.)

Back in the day there used to be a show called "The A-team". Not the movie with the guy from "The Hangover" you young puppies are thinking about, but the actual TV show. Every episode ended with Hannibal, the leader of the A-team, thinking of some elaborate plan to get them out of trouble.

They would be surrounded by enemy forces and Hannibal would make a tank out of a paper clip, a piece of gum, and a slinky. At the end of the show his tag line was, "I love it when a plan comes together." It wasn't "Man, if this slinky tank doesn't work, what are we going to do?"

Hannibal's belief in his plan was so powerful that his team followed him into battle, no matter what. They believed in him because he believed so strongly in himself. If for whatever crazy reason your plan doesn't work out, then you switch to a different plan, it's called adjusting. Make an adjustment. I got injured going after my plan A so I made another one.

Your plan A has three steps

1) Believe in yourself and your plan,
2) Put the work into it, and
3) Never let anyone convince you that you can't make a
slinky tank.

Jim Carrey

Jim Carrey revealed to James Lipton on "Inside the Actor's Studio" that when he was 15, he had to drop out of school to support his family. His father was an unemployed musician and as the family went from "lower middle class to poor," they eventually had to start living in a van. Carrey didn't let this stop him from achieving his dream of becoming a comedian: He went from having his dad drive him to comedy clubs in Toronto to starring in mega-blockbusters and being known as one of the best comedic actors of an era.

Most people stop knocking after the first door is closed, but Jim Carrey never lost sight of his Plan A. It's easy for us to lose focus on our dreams when adversity strikes.

What you must realize is that dreams without adversity are just fairytales. There will be opposition to your plan A. Just remember, if you believe in your Plan A and put in the work to achieve it you, won't have to worry about a Plan B.

Never count your dream out, if your Plan A is great then you don't have to worry about Plan B.

Chapter 10

TOLD YOU SO

- **Believe when others don't and you'll achieve when others won't.**
- **No one needs to buy into your dreams but you.**

I was on a ten year mission. From the ages of 16 to 26 I had this huge chip on my shoulder. Every time I practiced or played I would take that chip with me. Whenever I had to run or lift weights the chip was there. Most people with chips on their shoulders have an edge about them. They never seem satisfied with what they accomplish or how far they've come. I think I know the reason why.

My chip started from the very first person that told me I could never be a basketball player. It then slowly started to get bigger with every negative comment, every slight, and every person that laughed as I awkwardly tried to put this orange ball I became obsessed with into a ten foot high basket.

As I got older and better the chip didn't go anywhere. I was still angry at the people that doubted me. I couldn't believe they didn't think I would be successful. I was going to not only show them they were wrong but I was going to continually show them they were wrong over and over again.

It was going to become a big game of "I told you so" until they would be so sick of hearing those four words that they would eventually... Well, that's the part I didn't think through. I wasn't quite sure what would happen after I got the scholarship and the contract to play professionally.

Now what?

I spent ten years on this mission but now everyone
respected what I could do, and even supported what I was
doing. I started to realize that instead of proving people
wrong, I should just work to prove myself right. I knew that
eventually I would be able to accomplish all the goals with
basketball that I was chasing. Why would it matter that no
one else did? Who cares if the whole planet thought I
couldn't, as long as I believed I could? Isn't that all that
matters?

My mission, although it was one that helped me in a lot of
ways, had misplaced energy. Some of the energy I used to
keep that chip on my shoulder could have been used
differently. I had so much venom for those that doubted me,
that I couldn't enjoy playing the game. I felt like everything
was a direct challenge to who I was, as a person and a
player. It took me about four years after my playing days
were over to be able to actually have fun while playing
basketball. I couldn't enjoy the ride as much as I should have
because I was too busy trying to catch the cars in front of me
while simultaneously making sure the cars behind me would
never catch up.

Self-motivation is a funny thing. You need something to get
you out of bed in order to accomplish great things every day.
You need that voice pushing you past your comfort zone to a
level you never thought you could reach. I still have that
voice, but now the words are different.

Ten months ago I got the first proof of my book "The Power
of Positivity" in the mail. I still can't believe I held it in my
hands. It was a year and a half process, but it's finally come

to fruition. Holding that proof, the first thing I thought wasn't, "I told you so." It was, "I told you we could make this happen." That sentence was directed to me, by me, and not to anyone else.

Today, I set goals and put them as high up as possible. Every time I reach one, I prove myself right. It's a better feeling. Proving myself right reinforces the confidence I already had. It's not patting myself on the back as much as lifting my feet to get moving so I can do it again. Don't misplace your energy trying to prove everyone and their mother wrong; just prove yourself right.

DON'T THROW YOUR DREAMS IN A BUCKET WORKSHEET

I know the movie with Morgan Freeman and Jack Nicholson did pretty well at the box office but I disagree with the phrase "Bucket List" for a couple of reasons. First, and probably most important is, why do we only go after our dreams when the end is in sight? Do we really have to be near death to jump out of a plane, go on a safari, propose to the girl of our dreams, etc?

Second, a bucket (despite it meaning something else in their title) just holds something, be it water, the harmful chemicals we use on the kitchen floor, or whatever.

In this exercise we're not going to wait until we're about to die because, to be honest, we have no idea when that time is. We're going to make a To-Do List. That's right, things we want to accomplish while we can still enjoy them. LET'S GO!

I want you to write your To-Do List on anything that would make it legible. You can write down one thing or one hundred, it doesn't matter. The trick is, though, I want you to really give this some thought.

Don't just write down, "be a circus clown," if you have no intentions of being one. Turn off the television, the radio, and most important, your phone, and take ten minutes to make this happen.

The cool thing about this list is you can go back and add or subtract things depending on how you feel.

The last thing is, you need to put this somewhere you can find and access it easily. Every time you accomplish something on the "To-Do" list I want you to put a check by it. Deal? No cross-outs!!

1)

2)

3)

4)

5)

INFINITY)

Chapter 11

STRENGTH

- **What breaks you makes you; see the lesson in the loss.**
- **Make your solutions more important than your problems.**

In this day and age strength is measured physically more than mentally. You see some big muscle-headed guy lifting five hundred pounds incorrectly at your gym and what do you say, "Damn, that guy is strong!" You have no idea that same guy with the Speedo and dental floss tank top might fold under the slightest bit of adversity.

Yeah, he might be able to move your Mini Cooper by himself, but could he handle losing his job? Is he sitting on his couch crying into his protein shake after experiencing a setback? What we view as strong in our society is usually inaccurate.

For example the strongest human being I know is five foot two inches tall and definitely isn't winning any weight lifting competitions. Her name is Tina Thomas and to this day I have never met anyone who has displayed the kind of strength that she has through the years.

My mom raised five kids on her own (one of my brothers being Autistic) with very little money, and just the sheer determination and toughness to make sure her children had what they needed to be successful.

Her only goal in life was that we were fed, had a roof over our heads, and were good human beings. There was no such thing as a day off for her. A day off meant less money, and less money in our situation meant hungry kids. So off she went from one job to the next to make ends meet.

As a child I remember coming home from school with my siblings and my mom still at work from the night before. I couldn't figure it out. I had no idea how she was able to wake up every day and do the same thing over and over again.

Strength has little to do with size. Mahatma Gandhi wouldn't win any arm wrestling matches but how many of us could endure what he did to stand up for what he believed in? Would you March in Birmingham Alabama during the civil rights movement like Martin Luther King and thousands of other people did, both black and white, knowing the opposition that you were going to face?

It's mental strength and toughness that allows ordinary people to overcome extraordinary obstacles.

Adversity is a test that all of us have failed at one time or another. We all have had obstacles that we felt we weren't strong enough to move. Growing up, my mom would take us to church all the time and I remember being told the Bible said faith could move mountains.

Faith is a synonym for hope, trust, or belief. That could be in a person, thing, religion, etc. So, if you believe you can overcome something, nothing should be able to stop you from doing it.

If you're looking for strength, look inside of you and you'll see that you're a lot stronger than you could ever imagine.

OPRAH

She is one of the richest, most successful people in the world today, but Winfrey didn't always have it so easy. She grew up in Milwaukee, Wisconsin, and was repeatedly molested by her cousin, uncle and a family friend. She eventually ran away from home, and at age 14 gave birth to a baby boy who died shortly afterward.

But Winfrey's tragic past didn't stop her from becoming the force she is today. She excelled as an honors student in high school, and won an oratory contest that secured her a full college scholarship. Now, the entrepreneur and celebrity has the admiration of millions and a net worth of $2.9 billion.

Imagine if Oprah would have let her past determine her present? There would be no Oprah. In life you have to understand one basic fact, the only thing we have control over is the right now. We can't go forward or backward.

MY CHALLENGE TO YOU

I DARE YOU

I dare you to not be a product of your past. I dare you to break the mold that society so badly wants to put you in. I dare you to block out all the white noise in your life that makes you doubt your self worth. I dare you to start believing in you.

I dare you to stand on your own two feet. I dare you to stop worrying about who's behind you or who's in front of you. I dare you to be great even on the days you feel anything but. I dare you to change the world.

This isn't a blog, it's a challenge. People who achieve greatness are harder to find than Bigfoot these days and I think I know why. When we're younger we challenge each other all the time. One of our goofy friends would tell us we couldn't do something and, next thing you know, we would try to prove them wrong. Now this didn't always turn out in our favor, but it was the challenge that drove us. If our tongue ended up sticking to the frozen pole in front of the school, so be it.

These days we don't challenge ourselves enough. We stay in the middle of the pack, unwilling to run ahead. Leaving the pack behind would take extra work. It would involve getting out of our comfort zone. That's what separates the good from the great - the ability to deal with that discomfort and push forward despite it. So what are you going to do?

Are you going to wake up today and strive to be average?

Are your goals so low that you'll never have to stretch to reach them? Or are you going to challenge yourself to be more? The choice is yours.

I had a conversation with one of my younger coaches yesterday about goal setting. I told him to write down goals so big that they scare him. When your goals make you nervous, you know you're on the right track. If no one else will dare you to be great, I'll take the challenge right now. Because the greater we are as individuals, the greater we'll be as a planet.

BONUS QUOTES:

- *Never let the ones around you ground you; dream big.*

- *Don't waste time dreaming for someone else; focus on your own.*

- *Tomorrow is just a wish; focus on today.*

- *We create our fears, which means we also control them.*

- *The master of his fears will never be a servant to them.*

- *Quitting is an effortless act, which is why so many do it.*

- *Quitting is the only answer for those that question what they're made of.*

- *Quitting is an easy solution for those unwilling to face their problems.*

- *No storm should ever make you question if the sun will shine again.*

- *When no task is too small, no dream will ever be too big.*

- *Allow yourself to be yourself; life's too short to be anybody else.*

- *The only shoes you should be trying to fill are your own.*

- *You can't get ahead by looking behind, focus on the now.*

- *Even the best ears sometimes become deaf due to stubbornness.*

- *The negative carousel only stops when you decide to get off it.*

- *It's easy to find the wrong because the right is usually hidden behind it.*

- *Positivity cannot survive without consistency.*

- *Failure is a necessary pit stop on the road to greatness.*

- *Who you are when the sun is shining should be the same when it rains.*

- *Your last loss shouldn't stop you from your next win.*

- *You can always find the problems you're looking for.*

- *Be thankful for each breath and the opportunity to breathe it.*

- *Don't leave your chance up to chance, work for what you want.*

- *There will always be another excuse but there may not be another opportunity.*

- *Part of the battle is knowing that you've prepared for it.*

- *Love why you do, and what you do will be that much more rewarding.*

- *Don't chase your dreams; work until they get tired of running away.*

- *Your mind will quit before your body does.*

- *You can waste a lot of time waiting for the perfect time to take action.*

- *You can't cheat the game of life, you either live it or you don't.*

- *When your moment comes you should already be waiting for it.*

- *The storm with no warning is the one you must prepare for.*

- *Impact someone's life that can't directly impact yours.*

- *There are those that wait and those that work; choose*

wisely.

- *You'll miss every opportunity you don't see; be aware.*

- *Learn from what broke you and it will never break you again.*

- *Never disrespect the journey by not appreciating the destination.*

- *The mind is limited, put your heart into what you want.*

- *Even the darkest days cannot conceal the light inside us.*

- *You can't lock in to what you want without locking out what you don't.*

- *No one ever doubts the realist.*

- *Realistic dreams aren't dreams at all.*

- *Fear can turn the biggest dream into the smallest memory.*

- *Never let your dream get clouded by someone else's interpretation of it.*

- *Every path to the top starts from the bottom; have patience.*

- *A dream without opposition is a fairytale.*

- *Sometimes what you like must be sacrificed in order to get what you love.*

- *No challenge is as great as the one in your mind; believe to achieve.*

- *Time is like a cup you can fill it with whatever you choose, so choose wisely.*

- *Your problems are the first clues to your solutions.*

- *The moment you believe it's impossible it will be exactly that.*

- *Everyone wants to be great until they realize what greatness entails.*

- *Tomorrow depends on today, make the most of it.*

- *If you don't believe in you, expect others to follow your lead.*

- *You'll never solve the problem you don't allow yourself to see.*

- *Don't let fear put a ceiling on your success,*

- *Failure is just a pit stop on the road to success; don't let it slow you down.*

- *You can't live your life without loving it first.*

- *Don't worry about proving others wrong; prove yourself right.*

- *Opportunity has a way of finding those working hard for it.*

- *A life without purpose will always be in search of passion.*

- *Proving them wrong is temporary but proving you're right is forever.*

- *Words without actions will never accomplish dreams.*

- *If you're not learning from the loss, you'll never turn it into a win.*

- *Fear can either drive you or undermine you; the choice is yours.*

- *Bigger dreams take bigger actions.*

- *Nothing can stop you without your consent.*

- *If you're afraid to stand, be prepared to fall.*

- *There is no normal; there's who you are and who others want you to be.*

- *You'll never find what you refuse to see; be honest with yourself.*

- *Don't be a prisoner of your past, be a product of your present.*

- *Who you were then was necessary to discover who you are now.*

- *Your purpose isn't hiding; it's waiting to be found.*

- *There will always be room on the road less travelled.*

- *Dreamers don't waste time being realistic.*

- *The best version of you should be today.*

- *Each step taken is another step conquered; embrace the journey.*

- *In every mistake awaits a lesson.*

- *Fear is powerless without your consent.*

- *When your actions match your aspirations good things happen.*

- *Don't be afraid of being great; be afraid of not knowing you are.*

- *Challenge yourself every day and no day will ever be boring.*

- *Your path will take you as far as your work ethic is willing to travel.*

- *Gratitude isn't part time, appreciate each breath the moment you take it.*

- *Don't fault people for doubting your dreams; fault yourself for listening.*

- *Don't curse the heavens if you're putting yourself through hell.*

- *Time can turn a bad habit into a bad routine.*

- *Don't start today worrying about tomorrow; be present.*

- *You can't stick the landing unless you actually jump.*

- *Dreamers have a funny way of making the impossible, possible.*

- *Confidence comes from repeatedly proving yourself right, not others wrong.*

- *Don't sell your dreams short by not paying attention to them.*

- *You can't take your dream with you when you're gone; do it now.*

- *Don't waste time trying to make the blind see your vision.*

- *You must first know what's holding you down in order to lift yourself up.*

- *It's not what you have; it's what you'll leave behind that's important.*

- *Don't let your past define your present.*

- *Never let what they say stop you from what you do.*

- *Those that fear greatness will never attain it.*

- *Don't let the possibility of losing affect the probability of winning.*

- *Never fear the jump, fear not jumping at all.*

- *If you can see what you want to be, you can be what you want to be.*

- *The greater the dream, the greater the opposition.*

ACKNOWLEDGEMENTS AND THANK YOU'S

I would like to first thank my mother, Tina Thomas, for making her only dream in life to be raising her kids the right way. Thanks, Mom, for all your sacrifice. We love you more than words can express. I would like to thank my amazing wife Melissa for supporting a dream chaser no matter how outrageous the dream, and for being the best mom in the world, hands down. (I'm biased!) I want to thank my west coast mom and mother-in-law Janice Mitchell for your love. I would like to thank my brothers who have influenced me, each in their own way. Ron for being the father figure in our lives. Robert for coming into our lives and being such a great mentor to me. Craig for helping me understand that being different is a good thing and should be celebrated. Romont for making me tougher through our secret battles that Mom couldn't know about. Tony for being a fellow dreamer. My little sister, Alicia, a.k.a the family's world traveler, and my older sister, Jackie.

I would like to also thank my brother-in-law, Andy, and my sister-in-law, Jamilia, welcome to our crazy (in a great way) family. I want to thank all my aunts, uncles and family that have shown me love throughout my life. My cousin, Carlos, for inspiring me to pick up a basketball, and to my friend Ray who planted the seed that I could one day get better at basketball.

My Crossroads Basketball family, thank you for helping me find my purpose. I love you all for not only believing in what we do but how we do it. Can't forget my two generals at Crossroads Basketball, Vinny Synol and Randy Jackson. You guys are the epitome of what we're about. Thank you for all that you do. Thanks to the wonderful Vicki White for editing my masterpiece. I love you mom. Thanks to Mr. Enthusiasm, Robert E. Criner, for writing the wonderful Forward and being a great mentor.

Thanks to Renzo Gracie for being an inspiration to all that cross your path, and to changing my life through Jiujitsu. Micheal Grey for his great testimonial. Thanks to my Renzo Gracie Denville family and Professor Sernack for being my home away from home.

To the Mantegna family and my Blair Academy family. My Oola family for inspiring me daily and penning such a great Forward. Joey P for helping me start my very first blog. The Stafford family, Hayes family, Kniffin family, Cavanaugh Family, Feltus Family, Korn Family, Lord Family, Ledesma Family, Faubert Family, Muller Family, Goldsberry Family, Real World Martial Arts Denville Family, Renzo Gracie NYC Family, Snyder Family, Baranowski Family, Abrahamsen Family, DeMasi Family, Breheny Family, Colston Family, Garay Family, Smith Family, Livingston Family, Pinsonault Family, D'Alessio family, Synol Family, Jackson Family, Endicott family, Hart Family, Walters Family, Kennedy Family, Civello Family, My Q Kettlebell Family, Padden family and my publicist/sis, Ally Padden. The Laguardias and the Stuckey Chiropractic Crew. All the awesome chiro's I met from the CSW conference. The good people at Urwa, and countless others that have helped me throughout this process.

To my social media crew, Maria Giacalone Sinclair, Ntellekt, Impowerr, Alex and Ani, Mia Praught, KK from UK, Tony Robbins, Annie Hawkins, Les Floyd, Emily Thomas, Jason Houck, Tracey Edwards, Alan Stein, Ed O Neil, Racheal and Dom from Warrior radio, Ricky Young, Al Givens, Sharkie Zartmen, Mya, Jen and Colin from Karmapants, and all my great friends that help spread the word through social media. The ever growing Oola Flock, and my friends from Vegas.

A special thanks to Kristen Rath Photography and Dahl House Design for their unbelievable work and patience on the cover, and author photo.
This page wouldn't be complete if I didn't save the last spot for my two fathers. Bobby Thomas despite only being alive for my first four years on earth, you have inspired me throughout my life with the countless stories of how much you gave back to the community of Passaic, and to those less fortunate. Your footprints are too big to follow so I will do my best to walk right beside them.

My second dad, Steve Mitchell, a real life cowboy in every sense of the word. You accepted me with open arms and gave me your blessing to marry your daughter. I know the two of you are smiling down at your grandson, Bryce, I love you with all my heart.

There are a million other people that I want to individually thank but I can't let the acknowledgement page be longer than the book, I love you all. Thank you!!

Made in the USA
Middletown, DE
26 November 2014